1001
THINGS
EVERY CHILD
SHOULD TRY TO DO,
BEFORE
CHILDHOOD
IS THROUGH!

DAVID GUDGEON

iUniverse, Inc.
New York   Bloomington

1001 things every child should try to do, before childhood is through!

Copyright © 2010 David Gudgeon

iUniverse books may be ordered through booksellers or by contacting:

iUniverse
1663 Liberty Drive
Bloomington, IN 47403
www.iuniverse.com
1-800-Authors (1-800-288-4677)

ISBN: 978-1-4401-9884-7 (pbk)
ISBN: 978-1-4401-9885-4 (ebk)

Printed in the United States of America

iUniverse rev. date: 1/4/2010

This book is dedicated to my youngest son Achilles, and his older brother Warren, whom I hope will have the chance to experience everything in this book and more as life has to offer it…

They say that the meek shall inherit the Earth, (it's true) and they do, every single day. But then we are all made to grow up, aren't we?

So hurry up before it's too late! The early years are the most precious years in which we are all filled with wonder and discovery. These are the true years of magic, and as we become older they are all but lost to us.

Time is the enemy, and as you become older, you are more and more aware of it in every moment. Never waste it if you can help it. There are too many people who give up on themselves and never even attempt to reach part of their potential.

But despair not! The truth is that you are never too old and never too young either. If you are older and have done many of these things, then experience them again through your children or try them yourself if you never did. If there are things here you have not done, then experience it with your children. So quit making excuses, the world is as big as it *seems* small, and full of opportunities for joy and discovery. There are many things here that cover a variety of age groups.

Experience is a far better teacher than any book, even this one. Children learn from *association*, not *pronunciation*. So isn't it time to associate? If you know anything, then you know that children mostly learn by example, so set one!

And if you happen to be a child and you are experimenting with some of the suggestions in this book all on your own, well then bless you.

I sincerely hope you enjoy yourself and find your way joyfully through every endeavor.

And be sure to always be safe and use caution. Remember that everything you do must be done properly and safely. Have adult supervision and proper protection and instruction if needed whenever trying anything new.

And don't let the length or occasional exoticness of the list discourage you. You do what you can, we can't all do everything.

Remember, there are many the world over who would be fortunate to even be able to own a book like this, let alone if they could actually read it. Some of the things listed here may even seem trivial, like riding a bike for example. While you sit there reading this it may interest you to know that as of the time of this writing more than half the world's population has never even used a telephone! There are too many things in life that we take for granted.

I for one as a child due to the circumstances by

which I grew up never went to a circus or a zoo, had a bike, or skates, or skateboard, or went Trick-or-Treating, or swimming, or had a birthday party, I couldn't even have milk or a bed to sleep in. There are many other things that are too much to list here, but you get the idea. There are children the world over who would be lucky to do five things from this list in their entire lives. Feel fortunate in whatever it is that you can do.

And if there are things that you want to try that are not in this book, well, don't let me stop you! There are many places to go, many things to see, and much more to experience on this tiny mud-ball of a planet than I could possibly list here.

This book is only a taste of the world.

Savor the flavor!

Remember, life doesn't stop until you do!

So, don't stop!

1. Keep a journal, so you can write down all the great memories you will have from trying many of the ideas in this book!

2. Learn to ride a bike.

3. If you are really good, try riding a unicycle.

4. If you can do that, then you can probably learn to ride a scooter.

5. Learn to swim.

6. Someday, you may get the chance to swim in ocean water, like on the beach.

7. Once you've mastered swimming, then it's safe to row a boat out on a lake.

8. It would be nice to pack a picnic lunch for that boat ride.

9. Go fishing once you've mastered rowing.

10. Clean and cook your own fish.

11. And since you can swim, next time you are at the pool try your hand at diving.

12. If you're cool with diving, perhaps you should try snorkeling.

13. And while you are so good in the boat, try a canoe.

14. If they are available, take a paddle boat out sometime.

15. Stand on your head.

16. Learn to roller-skate.

17. And if you could do that, then you can learn to inline-skate.

18. And if you did that, then you can certainly learn to ice-skate.

19. Since we are on the subject of wheels, why not learn to use a skateboard?

20. If that was fun, maybe you could try a mountain board, (like a skateboard but with really big wheels).

21. And if you can use a skateboard, why not a flowboard?

22. Then there's snakeboarding.

23. And sandboarding.

24. And kiteboarding.

25. Then there's traditional surfing if you get the chance.

26. And tow surfing.

27. There's wake skating.

28. And wake boarding.

29. There's water skiing.

30. And skimboarding.

31. And windsurfing to name a few.

32. Watch the fireflies deep in the night.

33. Catch some in a jar, (don't forget to let them go).

34. Find a caterpillar, keep him until he cocoons, then watch him transform into a butterfly and set him free.

35. Have a huge bubble bath!

36. Walk barefoot in the mud.

37. Play with invisible ink.

38. Collect sports cards.

39. Collect comic books.

40. Collect stamps.

41. Go to the zoo and take a picture of every animal.

42. Be sure to pet the animals at the petting area in the zoo.

43. And you may as well feed them too.

44. In fact, you may be able to volunteer at the zoo.

45. Start a scrapbook.

46. Keep a diary.

47. Make a list of things you like about yourself.

48. Make a list of things that make you happy.

49. Make a list of things that you dislike.

50. Curl up in a big comfortable chair with your favorite book and read the whole thing.

51. Own one of those ride on inflatable hoppers.

52. And a Sit and Spin.

53. Go to a circus.

54. When you are there, ride the elephant.

55. Ride the camel too if they have one.

56. And they almost always have a pony ride available, why not do that too?

57. Play circus sometime and make yourself up like a clown.

58. Quit a really bad habit that you have that you would be better off without.

59. Write a script for a TV show or movie.

60. Act the script out and film it.

61. If you can't film it, act it out as a play for relatives or friends.

62. Sing in front of an audience like on stage.

63. Learn to eat with chopsticks.

64. Visit a botanical garden.

65. Feed the squirrels; see if one will eat from your hand.

66. Feed a group of pigeons, walk around and drop the feed so they follow you around.

67. If there are no pigeons, perhaps you can feed some chickens.

68. Collect your own eggs.

69. Since it would be nice to visit a farm.

70. While we are on the farm, maybe you can ride a horse.

71. Perhaps you can visit a bee-farm & harvest your own honey.

72. Make someone a gift basket.

73. Learn to walk on a balance beam.

74. Jump around on a giant trampoline.

75. And a little trampoline too.

76. Play in a ball pit.

77. Race a go-cart.

78. Ride in a shopping cart.

79. Make your own ice-cream.

80. Fill ice trays with juice instead of water and make juice-cubes.

81. Try this with bits of fruit mixed in.

82. Maybe you might like to put some of those cubes in a blender with your favorite fruit and make your own smoothie.

83. Make your own gelatin.

84. And your own pudding too.

85. Make your own peanut butter.

86. Go sledding, (if you live somewhere with no snow, you might can do this in sand).

87. If you have access to both sand and snow, you may want to do both.

88. If you can sled, try snowboarding.

89. And why not skiing?

90. Go to a carnival and ride everything, even if it's scary.

91. Afterwards, sample all the carnival food.

92. And take a chance on every game.

93. Build your own snow globe.

94. Make your own candy apples.

95. Carve a pumpkin.

96. Jump in a big pile of leaves.

97. Wear a wig.

98. Own a megaphone.

99. Learn to juggle balls.

100. Then try juggling clubs.

101. Finally, try juggling rings.

102. And then there's always devil sticks.

103. And what about a Chinese yo-yo?

104. Or hat juggling?

105. Then there's mouth juggling.

106. And have you seen box juggling?

107. Finally, you may want to try scarf juggling.

108. If you are brave, there is always plate-spinning.

109. Learn to do cartwheels.

110. Lie in the grass late at night and stare up at the stars.

111. Lie in the grass in the day and pick out shapes in the clouds.

112. Study the different types of clouds and what they mean.

113. Run up and down the beach.

114. Bury yourself in the sand.

115. Dig for seashells.

116. Hold a seashell to your ear and see if you can hear the ocean.

117. Build a sandcastle.

118. Build a birdhouse.

119. Go to a pet store that lets you touch the animals, and touch them.

120. If they have exotic birds, let a parrot climb up on your shoulder.

121. Feed a flock of geese; see if they will eat from your hand.

122. Fly a kite.

123. Have a cake that is just for you.

124. Catch a frog, (don't forget to let him go).

125. Get a science kit and try all the experiments.

126. They have a kit for electrical experiments as well.

127. And let's not forget about the classic build a volcano kit!

128. Read a whole stack of comic books.

129. Light some fireworks.

130. Build a bottle rocket.

131. Take a hot air balloon ride.

132. Jump a ramp on your bike.

133. Own a bubble gum machine.

134. Flip over a log or a rock and look at the bugs underneath.

135. Dig a deep hole and see what is down there, (remember to fill it back up).

136. Go to your junior prom.

137. Go to your real prom.

138. Play miniature golf.

139. Play real golf.

140. Have a really huge birthday party.

141. Blow out all of the candles all by yourself.

142. Have a themed party.

143. Make your own invitations.

144. Build a glider plane.

145. Build a snowman.

146. Make snow angels.

147. Build an igloo.

148. Have a snowball fight.

149. Spend some time in a batting cage.

150. Spend some time on the golf driving range.

151. And the putting range.

152. Plant a tree.

153. Ride in a trolley car.

154. Make your own scrambled eggs.

155. Make some pancakes or waffles to go with them, (real ones, no toasters allowed).

156. Take your lovely breakfast food to your room and have breakfast in bed, (careful).

157. Have a nice bowl of mixed berries with some fresh whipped cream.

158. Go camping.

159. Start the campfire yourself.

160. Roast some wieners over an open fire.

161. Roast some marshmallows for desert while you are there.

162. Make up and tell a scary story around the campfire.

163. Look for and identify animal tracks.

164. Make a plaster cast of the tracks.

165. Go to the florist or a floral department in a store and sample smelling all the different flowers.

166. Learn to shoot a bow and arrow at a target.

167. Learn to shoot a slingshot at a target.

168. Learn to shoot a pellet gun at a target.

169. And finally, if you are safe enough, learn to shoot a b-b gun at a target.

170. Learn to read a clock with no numbers on it.

171. Watch wheat or corn being harvested.

172. Own a lava lamp.

173. Go trick-or-treating.

174. Play some tricks! (Not anything mean).

175. Make your own costume.

176. Have a Halloween party.

177. Wash a dog.

178. Groom the dog.

179. Try washing a cat, (good luck).

180. Go to a rodeo.

181. Go to a real professional baseball game.

182. Go to a real basketball game.

183. You may as well go to a real football game too.

184. And how about hockey? You may like that.

185. Or soccer even?

186. The next time there is a comet, go and watch it.

187. Watch for a meteor shower too.

188. See a lunar eclipse.

189. Witness a solar eclipse if you can.

190. Watch a beautiful sunrise.

191. And why not a sunset too?

192. It may be amazing to see a distant thunderstorm while you are watching the weather.

193. And don't forget to jump in the puddle!

194. Create a sculpture with paper mache.

195. Go to a horse race.

196. Go to a dog race.

197. Do some babysitting.

198. Make your own candles.

199. Make your own hard candy.

200. Heat some chocolate, and dip fruit in it.

201. Pick out your own dozen at a donut shop.

202. Write a story.

203. And illustrate the pictures for your story.

204. Learn an actual card trick and show your friends.

205. Get a magic kit and put on a whole show.

206. Make finger puppets.

207. Make shadow puppets.

208. Make some real puppets.

209. Try playing with a marionette.

210. Put on a puppet show.

211. Go to a professional puppet show.

212. Write a note in a bottle and throw it into the ocean.

213. Take first aid and CPR classes.

214. Visit an aquarium.

215. Watch the animal show there.

216. If they have an open pool for visitors, touch the sea animals inside of it.

217. Visit an art museum.

218. Always visit the gift shop in any museum.

219. Soak in a hot tub.

220. Sleep in a hammock.

221. Try your hand at a wind instrument.

222. Try a stringed instrument.

223. And best of all, try a percussion instrument.

224. Watch a parade and stand curbside.

225. Sit and watch a snowfall.

226. Try and catch the snowflakes on a clear piece of glass or plastic so you can examine the shapes.

227. Take a day off and go to a spa.

228. Start a garden, grow a food you like and eat it.

229. Plant some flowers too.

230. Make a nice rock garden to accompany it.

231. Go bird watching.

232. Have a slumber party.

233. Go to someone else's slumber party.

234. Try learning a foreign language.

235. Chop some firewood.

236. Attend a fireworks display.

237. Attend a monster truck show.

238. Press some apples and make your own apple juice.

239. Squeeze some oranges too!

240. Open a lemonade stand.

241. Have a yard sale.

242. Shop at some yard sales.

243. Go to the movies all day long and watch different films.

244. Go on a picnic.

245. Pick fruit from trees like apples or peaches or pears.

246. Pick your own berries.

247. Enter a walk-a-thon.

248. Ride on the back of a motorcycle.

249. You and a parent or friend learn Morse code,

and then talk to each other in the dark with flashlights.

250. Or try inventing your own code.

251. Walk through a field of sunflowers.

252. Fill a bunch of glasses with different levels of water and play them like an instrument with spoons.

253. Catch snowflakes on your tongue.

254. Make snowflake cutouts.

255. Own a set of Tinker-Toys.

256. And Lincoln Logs.

257. Put up a tent in the living-room or in your bedroom.

258. Light candles in the neck of a bottle so that as they melt they completely cover the bottle with wax.

259. Shovel snow.

260. Write a song.

261. Sing it for your family or friends.

262. Bake your own cookies from scratch.

263. Better yet, make your own fortune cookies.

264. Be sure to write some clever fortunes for them.

265. Now try muffins and cupcakes.

266. And finally, bake your own cake.

267. Learn to type, (without looking).

268. Organize and write your own personal newspaper.

269. Try out some stunts with your bike.

270. Spend an afternoon at the library and browse through the books, (no gaming on the computers).

271. See if you can volunteer there while you are at it.

272. Try spending an afternoon at the bookstore too; compare the experience.

273. Climb a tree.

274. Swing from a tree.

275. Swing out over a lake and dive-bomb in.

276. Play tug of war.

277. Build a tree house.

278. Visit an airport.

279. Ride in an airplane.

280. Interview a college athlete.

281. Make a pen pal with someone overseas.

282. Throw a football through a tire-swing.

283. Slide down the pole in a firehouse.

284. Go to a skate park and learn some tricks.

285. Go to a pumpkin patch on Halloween and pick your own pumpkin.

286. Visit a haunted house while it's in season.

287. Take a hayride.

288. Paint a picture.

289. Learn the birthstones.

290. Wear a couple of thick sweatshirts, and let a kitten climb you.

291. Watch a classic show from the golden era of television, (around the 1950s).

292. Play in a fountain.

293. Feed a baby animal with a bottle.

294. Feed a human baby with a bottle.

295. And if that's not messy enough, spoon feed a baby.

296. Mow a lawn.

297. Skip rocks in a lake.

298. Enter a pie eating contest.

299. Ride an electric scooter.

300. Go to an antique car show.

301. Build your own ham radio.

302. Learn to sew.

303. Make your own article of clothing and wear it.

304. Learn to bowl, tenpin and candlepin if you have access to both.

305. Play a real pinball machine.

306. Play pool on a real billiards table.

307. Spend a day having a conversation with someone who is really very old and ask them about what it was like when they were your age.

308. Get a paper route or some other age appropriate job.

309. Fill a bunch of paper plates with different colored paints and dip your hands and feet in them to paint on a large piece of paper.

310. Mix a whole bunch of different sodas together at the fountain and invent your own flavor.

311. Make your own milkshakes at home.

312. Eat raw cookie dough.

313. Grow an avocado in a glass of water.

314. Spend the day experimenting with an old record player.

315. Take extreme close-up photos of insects and flowers.

316. Learn to play chess.

317. Temporarily tattoo yourself with henna.

318. Make and bake your own pie.

319. Make some mud pies while you are on the subject.

320. Wash a car.

321. Dress up and go to a nice restaurant.

322. Go to a play afterwards.

323. Or even take in a musical.

324. And why not see a ballet as well?

325. Learn to tell military time.

326. Learn to read sheet music.

327. Make your own pizza.

328. Play with a remote control car.

329. And a remote control helicopter.

330. And a remote control plane too.

331. Lastly, a remote control boat.

332. Play bingo!

333. Learn to draw.

334. Build something with Lego's that didn't come with the instructions.

335. Create something with modeling clay.

336. Paint Easter eggs.

337. Decoratively paint and detail an egg, (like a Faberge egg).

338. Decorate a Christmas tree.

339. Decorate a tree that is outdoors.

340. Decorate the house on every holiday at least once.

341. Let a cat fall asleep in your lap.

342. Ride in a police car with the siren on and not even be in trouble.

343. Shoot twenty baskets in a row from the foul line.

344. Have monogrammed pencils with your name on them.

345. And a monogrammed pen too.

346. Watch an animal being born.

347. Make your own tie-dye t-shirt.

348. Make your own donuts at home.

349. Take a tour of a factory that processes food.

350. If you can, take a tour of a bottling company too.

351. It would be nice to see a factory that makes machinery or consumer goods too.

352. It would be interesting to see printing presses in action like at a newspaper company.

353. Ride in a limo.

354. Learn to drive a car.

355. Put together a model train set.

356. Set up a model race track and race.

357. Launch a model rocket.

358. Spend a whole day where you chew gum the whole time.

359. Don't forget to blow big bubbles with the gum.

360. Try sushi.

361. Play with a yo-yo.

362. Play with a Frisbee.

363. Play with a boomerang.

364. Have ice cream for breakfast.

365. Have cereal for dinner.

366. Make a sundial.

367. Join a little league team.

368. Join a soccer team.

369. And youth basketball.

370. Learn to wrestle.

371. Build a model car.

372. Build a model plane.

373. Play marbles.

374. Play jacks.

375. Experiment with woodworking.

376. Milk a cow.

377. Milk a goat.

378. Make a lasso and teach yourself how to rope something.

379. Go to a book reading at the library.

380. Read a book to someone much younger than you.

381. Change a diaper.

382. Try some old video games from when they first came out in the 1970s and 1980s.

383. Learn to throw darts.

384. Make your own stuffed animal.

385. Play Laser Tag.

386. Have a huge squirt gun fight.

387. And have a water balloon fight too.

388. While we are on the subject of water, visit a water park.

389. Build a gingerbread house.

390. And bake some gingerbread men.

391. Shop at a flea market.

392. Play hopscotch.

393. Play jump rope.

394. And hopper rope.

395. Make your own soap.

396. Go to a wrestling match.

397. Eat breakfast for every meal for one day.

398. Walk around on a pair of stilts.

399. Attend a stockcar race.

400. And a drag race.

401. Let's not forget to see a motocross race either.

402. And then there's quad racing too.

403. Go exploring in the woods.

404. Go exploring by a creek.

405. Visit a Christmas village.

406. Take computer lessons; learn how to actually use computer programs, (not games).

407. Learn to repair or work on a computer, find out how they work and why.

408. Experiment with a microscope.

409. Experiment with a telescope.

410. Watch an annual rubber duck race.

411. Have a *me* day where everything you do all day is all about you.

412. Visit an air museum.

413. Visit a children's museum.

414. And a science museum.

415. Visit an observatory, (there may be one at a local university).

416. Try to get on an athletic team at school.

417. Try to get on the band too.

418. And if you have gotten good with an instrument, try to form your own band.

419. Join a club.

420. Maybe you could even create a club of your own.

421. Go to a comic book convention.

422. Go to an antique and vintage toy convention.

423. And see an antiques auction too.

424. Eat a totally *not* nutritious sandwich made with marshmallow and chocolate spreads.

425. Play hacky sack.

426. Pick things up with your toes.

427. Go to a construction site and watch the big machines.

428. Get a subscription to a magazine.

429. Write your own comic strip.

430. Ride in a glass elevator.

431. Visit an antique railroad.

432. Ride on a real train.

433. Have your own shopping spree.

434. Volunteer in a homeless shelter.

435. Pop a sheet of bubble wrap.

436. Make a dream-catcher.

437. Go to a theme park.

438. Learn to do your basic math without a calculator.

439. Play with a Rubik's Cube puzzle and learn how to solve it, (without taking it apart).

440. Sleep in the top bunk.

441. Sleep in a waterbed.

442. Go away to a summer camp.

443. Play hide and seek.

444. Stand up to a bully. You don't necessarily have to fight to stand up to someone who is pushing you or someone else around, but do stand up for yourself.

445. Enter a junior achievement contest.

446. Order some fancy deserts and candies from a catalog.

447. Swim at an indoor pool.

448. Take Karate lessons, (or whatever martial arts or self defense program you prefer).

449. Spend a day alone with nature and in complete solitude to think about who you are and who you want to be.

450. Get involved in an environmental cleanup project.

451. Own and care for a reptile.

452. And then perhaps a rodent such as a guinea pig or hamster.

453. And then a bird.

454. Finally, some sort of mammal like a cat or a dog.

455. Visit a local television station.

456. And a local radio station.

457. Have a colored bulb in a lamp in your room.

458. Ride on a *real* merry-go-round.

459. Ride on a *real* miniature train.

460. Watch an egg being hatched.

461. Observe a wedding.

462. Observe a funeral.

463. Have a fish in a tank.

464. Have a coming of age party like a sweet 16 or a Bar/Bat Mitzvah for example.

465. Pump gas.

466. Have class pictures taken.

467. Ring a church bell.

468. Compete in a race.

469. Make a fort or a clubhouse out of a huge box like the kind a refrigerator or a stove come packed in.

470. Have an ant farm.

471. Have a worm farm.

472. Make your own potato chips.

473. Make a time capsule, bury it, and dig it up when you are grown.

474. Help paint a house.

475. Have an I.D. card.

476. Learn to whistle.

477. Take a bath and a shower at the same time.

478. Own a pair of binoculars.

479. Use them to do some bird watching.

480. A periscope would be fun to own also.

481. And why not a kaleidoscope?

482. Have a gift card to shop with.

483. Do something nice that gets your picture in the paper.

484. Participate in a parade.

485. Learn to identify the constellations at night.

486. Read the complete Aesop's fables, and understand the morals.

487. Have a set of business cards.

488. Have a set of address labels.

489. Take a trip within your country that brings you far from home.

490. If you can, take a trip to a foreign land.

491. Have a professional portrait session.

492. Earn an academic achievement award.

493. Win a trophy.

494. Have a keepsake box that you keep personal items in.

495. Keep a photo album.

496. Learn to write good cursive.

497. Learn sign language.

498. Put together a giant jigsaw puzzle.

499. Make your own jigsaw puzzle.

500. Learn Roman numerals.

501. Run through a corn maze.

502. Own a pocket knife.

503. Watch a silent movie.

504. Visit an animal shelter.

505. They may let you volunteer there too.

506. Drop water balloons out of a high window, (not as a practical joke, don't hurt or upset anyone).

507. Own a pair of really cool looking sunglasses.

508. And a really nice hat.

509. Yell into a fan.

510. Learn to use a fire extinguisher.

511. Catch bugs.

512. Read classic books.

513. Record yourself singing.

514. Make your own fried doe.

515. And your own taffy.

516. Make your own greeting cards for the holidays.

517. Help an elderly or pregnant person load their groceries in their car and refuse any tip.

518. Experiment with a crystal growing kit.

519. And a robot kit.

520. Visit a windmill farm.

521. Attend an ice cream festival.

522. Attend a real recording session.

523. Own a model of the constellations.

524. Visit a real confectionary shop.

525. And a real pastry shop.

526. Try foods from another person's culture.

527. Read the biography of a successful business person.

528. And read about a famous scientist.

529. And perhaps read about an athlete.

530. Or even a biography of a famous person from history.

531. Have a board game night.

532. Learn to play cards.

533. Check out the state fair.

534. Enter the contests while you are there.

535. Play the games too.

536. Visit a magic shop.

537. See a real magician live on stage.

538. Go to a themed restaurant.

539. Work on the school paper.

540. If your school takes submissions for a publication, get in on the act.

541. Run for class president.

542. And student body president.

543. Go for a week with no television or video games, (some of the most successful people will tell you that they neither watch television nor play video games, they are too busy living real lives to watch fake ones on TV or in a game).

544. Go for a week with no soda pop or sports drinks, drink water and real juice instead and see how you feel.

545. Get involved in a theatre project.

546. Keep an autograph book.

547. Take a gymnastics class.

548. And some dance lessons.

549. Go to a bodybuilding competition.

550. Listen to some old time radio shows from before there was television.

551. Roast nuts on an open fire.

552. Get involved in a recycling program.

553. Try a real natural soda, made with natural sugar and no corn syrup or food colorings in it.

554. Check out the community events calendar at your local library.

555. Check out the parks and recreations calendar too.

556. Exercise for an hour every day.

557. Practice running and jogging.

558. Jump hurdles.

559. Climb a chain-link fence.

560. Visit a national park.

561. Build a squirrel feeder.

562. And a bird feeder.

563. Visit a real prison.

564. Visit a rehab center.

565. Volunteer at an elderly home.

566. Attend a professional ice show.

567. Make an ice cream float.

568. Check out your local ROTC programs.

569. See what a real blacksmith does in person.

570. Build an item of armor out of chainmaille like in ancient times.

571. Enter a spelling bee.

572. Earn an honor roll.

573. Learn to make balloon animals.

574. Go to a Senior Olympics.

575. Go to the Special Olympics.

576. Visit with terminally ill children.

577. Have a pillow fight.

578. Play ping-pong.

579. Play badminton.

580. Try real tennis.

581. And lacrosse.

582. Examine the intricacies of knot tying.

583. Get a treat from an ice cream truck.

584. Become an avid reader, many people set serious limitations on themselves because they never learn to read at an adult level. Being a good reader could be the turning point on how bright a person's future shines.

585. Visit an aerospace museum.

586. Stick up for someone smaller than you.

587. Tutor someone younger than you.

588. Write a mini biography about yourself.

589. See a laser show.

590. Watch a live orchestra in concert.

591. Go to an opera.

592. Watch a live jazz band.

593. And see a live a-capella group.

594. Learn to do gimp.

595. Weave a basket.

596. Read a book on how things work.

597. Investigate a world atlas.

598. Pop your own popcorn.

599. Make a stained glass window hanging.

600. Make a wind chime.

601. Own a nice suit or dress.

602. And a nice pair of shoes to match.

603. Go on an Easter egg hunt.

604. And a scavenger hunt.

605. Learn your times tables.

606. Participate on a debating team.

607. Take novelty photos of yourself with Santa or the Easter Bunny for example.

608. Own a camera.

609. Have a giant set of crayons.

610. And a set of colored pencils.

611. Learn table etiquette.

612. And take elocution lessons.

613. Learn to do the laundry.

614. And be able to fold it properly.

615. Learn to iron too.

616. Own a piggy bank or some other savings bank.

617. Have a savings account.

618. Get a class ring from your school.

619. And a letterman jacket.

620. And fill that jacket with your achievements.

621. Own a piece of jewelry with your birthstone on it.

622. Go sailing.

623. Milk a coconut.

624. Go to the top of the tallest building you can find and look down from the top floor.

625. Climb the stairs of that building to get to the top.

626. Go on a treasure hunt.

627. Watch a professional dance performance like ballroom or tap.

628. Own a metal detector.

629. Go beach combing with it.

630. Pay a visit to the city dump.

631. And stop by the city's water treatment plant.

632. Own several pairs of different colored socks.

633. Visit a big greenhouse.

634. And check out a granary.

635. See a troop of performing Chinese acrobats.

636. Make your own hot cocoa.

637. And bake your own bread.

638. Build a ship in a bottle.

639. Watch a live demolition in person.

640. Shop at a farmers market.

641. Visit your state or local capital building.

642. Watch a classic movie.

643. Own a nice watch.

644. Have a piece of jewelry with your name or your initials on it.

645. Own some personal monogrammed stationary.

646. And have a set of rubber stamps for your stationary.

647. Have a growth chart.

648. Check out a recycling facility.

649. When you sit down for a meal, think about where the food came from and what effort went into obtaining it and preparing it.

650. Drive a golf cart.

651. Visit a real arcade.

652. Eat fresh fruit every day.

653. Eat fresh vegetables too.

654. Brush and care for your teeth in a daily routine, (honestly, I know people younger

than me that have lost nearly all their teeth from neglect)!

655. See if it is possible to observe your parents at their work so you can see what it is that they do.

656. Shear a sheep.

657. Brush a horse.

658. Watch a dog round up and guide sheep.

659. Help work a barbecue.

660. Clean rain gutters.

661. Go to a clam bake.

662. Help to change a tire.

663. Visit a real bakery.

664. Visit the butchers too.

665. Watch a snake eat.

666. Make your own mask.

667. Own a little safe.

668. Walk on a rope bridge.

669. Cross a suspension bridge.

670. Climb a rope like in some gym classes.

671. Take a tour of a battleship.

672. Take a tour of a clipper ship.

673. Ride in a speedboat.

674. Own a wallet/purse.

675. Practice taking aptitude tests.

676. Learn to do word search puzzles.

677. And crossword puzzles too.

678. Roll down a hill.

679. Roll in the grass.

680. Blow bubbles.

681. Make huge bubbles with a bubble wand.

682. Play with a bubble machine.

683. Have a pizza party.

684. Make cheese breads in the broiler or toaster oven.

685. Make cinnamon and or sugar toast in the broiler.

686. Make your own peanut butter.

687. Own a funny looking cup.

688. And a crazy straw to go with it.

689. Play with silly string.

690. Learn how to write a proper essay.

691. Receive flowers.

692. Give someone flowers.

693. Press flowers in a book.

694. Learn to fill out a checkbook.

695. Have a calendar book to schedule activities.

696. Have a notebook for events and itinerary.

697. Have and complete a chore list.

698. Keep a little black book with phone numbers instead of relying on the memory in a cell phone.

699. Own a tool set.

700. Make a mosaic with little rocks, etc…

701. Build a terrarium.

702. Make a sand sculpture.

703. And try sand painting too.

704. And then there's rock painting.

705. Try finger painting.

706. Paint with sliced fruits and veggies.

707. Graduate to watercolor.

708. Build something with Popsicle sticks.

709. Have a Play-Dough Fun Factory.

710. And you can even make your own play-dough.

711. Stay up late one Saturday night.

712. Build a collage.

713. Take the graduation walk.

714. Blow away dandelion seeds.

715. Taste water from the ocean, (don't drink it).

716. Make chalk drawings on the sidewalk.

717. Own an Etchasketch.

718. Own a Spirograph.

719. And an Erector Set.

720. Have a collection of magnets.

721. Randomly look up a new word every day in a dictionary.

722. Own a dictionary, (you would be surprised how many people don't).

723. Make your own jewelry.

724. Help a wounded animal.

725. Play with stacking cups.

726. Enter a talent show.

727. Visit a sick friend.

728. Sign a friends cast.

729. Earn what you need and want, never steal it.

730. Examine someone else's religion.

731. Learn to take care of your own hair.

732. "Ask for nothing, refuse nothing", (a quote from St. Francis de Sales) which is a good philosophy to try and live by.

733. Play volley ball.

734. Look at yourself in the mirror and say, "I am a beautiful person", (looks have nothing to do with this).

735. Have a handicap experience, (for example, see what it is like to eat a meal blindfolded, etc…).

736. Visit a courthouse and sit in on a trial.

737. Jump up and down on a moving elevator.

738. Go the wrong way on an escalator, (stop if they tell you).

739. Make your own calendar.

740. Own a set of walkie-talkies.

741. And then a set of two way radios.

742. Have a big bunch of helium balloons.

743. Experiment with a solar power science kit.

744. Play horse shoes.

745. And lawn darts.

746. Play croquet.

747. And ladder ball.

748. And also for the backyard, try bocce ball.

749. Set up a backyard water slide.

750. Watch the live lobsters in a seafood restaurant or supermarket.

751. Build a house of cards.

752. Go to a family reunion.

753. Get a big family photo.

754. Create your own board game.

755. Wrap gifts for others.

756. Write a letter to your congressman.

757. Learn napkin folding.

758. Learn the order of the planets in our Solar System.

759. Watch some old cheesy monster movies.

760. Try your hand at calligraphy.

761. Try some fondue.

762. Own a junior spy kit.

763. Enter a science fair.

764. Make your own mobile.

765. Experiment with a computer graphics program, (draw on your computer).

766. Play air hockey.

767. And foosball.

768. Participate in a secret Santa, or something like it.

769. Have your own family contest.

770. Watch an equestrian competition.

771. Go to a dog park.

772. Go to a dog show.

773. Go to a cat show.

774. Draw a picture of your dream house.

775. Own a flashlight.

776. Own a laser pointer, (be responsible with it).

777. Own a portable music device.

778. Taste some exotic fruits.

779. Go to a motorcycle rally.

780. Check out a boat show.

781. Watch a tractor pull.

782. And a demolition derby.

783. Visit a real health food store.

784. Visit a power plant.

785. And a military base.

786. Go on school field trips.

787. Study an ancient culture of your choice.

788. Make snow cones.

789. Mix your own fruit punch.

790. Go to a stock car race.

791. And a formula one race.

792. Study classical music.

793. In fact, listen to all types of music. Do not limit yourself to only one type.

794. Join a track team.

795. Learn to read food labels.

796. And learn to understand what those labels mean, know what you are putting in your body and how it affects you.

797. Read classic poetry.

798. Trace your family tree.

799. Study your family history.

800. Examine your true cultures ancestry as well as you can.

801. Own something personalized that's just for you.

802. Have an article of clothing that's embroidered with your name or initials.

803. Learn to do number puzzles.

804. Build a fort.

805. Play Twister.

806. Play dominos.

807. Stack dominos.

808. Write a letter to yourself that you will open and read when you are an adult.

809. Own a pair of cowboy boots.

810. And a cowboy hat.

811. Ride on a human transport, (you know, one of those two wheeled electric carts you stand in).

812. Ride a bicycle built for two with a friend.

813. Study the Constitution.

814. Watch the Harvest Moon.

815. Play Scrabble.

816. Experiment with a fingerprinting kit.

817. Practice knocking down tin cans with baseballs.

818. Go to a Sci-Fi convention.

819. Try baton twirling.

820. Play a practical joke on someone, (don't be mean about it).

821. Assemble a sticker book.

822. Make your own flip book.

823. Make a paperclip chain.

824. Practice yoga.

825. Learn meditation, learn to calm yourself.

826. Own a copy of the Guinness Book of World Records.

827. Make a rubber band ball.

828. And a big foil ball.

829. Learn to repair your own bike.

830. Get a t-shirt autographed by your class and friends when you graduate from a school.

831. Own a copy of your yearbook.

832. Go to a fiesta.

833. Study basic anatomy.

834. Study geology.

835. Own a rock tumbler to make the geology more fun.

836. Visit a hobby shop.

837. Visit an antique store.

838. See if you can meet the local mayor.

839. And your local representative.

840. Taste test at every local pizzeria and see which is best.

841. Practice your posture.

842. Play tag.

843. Play dodge ball.

844. Gather wildflowers.

845. Visit your nation's capital.

846. Go to a gem and precious metals show.

847. Eat a big piece of watermelon and spit the seeds.

848. See a King Richards Fair.

849. Make your own mac-and-cheese from scratch.

850. Make a macaroni sculpture.

851. Design and build your own picture frame for your favorite photo.

852. Build a shadow box.

853. Get pictures taken in a photo booth.

854. Have a caricature artist draw your picture.

855. Join a college fraternity.

856. Learn to use a hula-hoop.

857. Learn to play a ukulele.

858. Put the two together and learn to do the hula!

859. Own a goblet.

860. Own a crown or a tiara!

861. Have a costume party.

862. Cover yourself with temporary tattoos.

863. See a deer in the wild.

864. Use a pogo stick.

865. Try some spray-on hair color.

866. Play with glow sticks.

867. Burn your own CDs.

868. Experiment with foam art.

869. Own an arts and crafts kit.

870. Learn needlepoint.

871. Knitting might be interesting too.

872. And if you liked that, you may like crocheting.

873. If you own a dog, teach it some tricks.

874. Marvel at a rainbow.

875. Practice logic puzzles.

876. Own a compass.

877. Own a pair of Heelys or some other shoe with built in skates.

878. Make sock puppets.

879. Play with Chinese Fortune Sticks.

880. Try quilting.

881. Take a pottery class.

882. Play with tanogram's.

883. Own a globe of the Earth.

884. Own a globe of the Moon.

885. Own a local map of where you live.

886. Own a map of your country.

887. Own a map of the world.

888. Have a library card.

889. Always try free samples.

890. Track down and examine some old photographs.

891. Have a souvenir from anyplace you visit.

892. Own a sharks tooth and/or some other common fossils.

893. Learn your weights and measures.

894. Visit a comedy club.

895. Write and perform your own stand up routine.

896. Keep a dream diary.

897. Make up your own secret code.

898. Own a magic 8-ball.

899. Do a dissection in biology.

900. Have a rubber duck.

901. Build a scale model of a house or a building.

902. Keep a houseplant.

903. And defiantly a Venus flytrap.

904. Attend a garden show.

905. Have a Slinky.

906. Have a prism.

907. And a magnifying glass.

908. Get accustomed to reading the newspaper, preferably one that has national and international news, not just local stuff.

909. Own a hermit crab.

910. Work with an engraving kit.

911. And a wood burning kit.

912. Try leather-craft.

913. Own a collection of seashells.

914. Experiment with a physics set.

915. And a hydraulics set.

916. Build a model engine.

917. Try paint by number.

918. And draw by number.

919. Make your own soap.

920. Own a set of stencils.

921. Own a whistle.

922. And a water whistle.

923. And a slide whistle.

924. And a harmonica.

925. Learn napkin folding, (kind of like origami).

926. Try painting ceramic plates.

927. Own a flag of your country.

928. Color a velvet poster.

929. Play with silly-putty.

930. Own a gyroscope.

931. Every kid should have a paddleball.

932. And own a catchers mitt.

933. It is nice to have an assortment of sports balls too.

934. Every kid should own a first aid kit.

935. And a wagon to carry things.

936. Own an audio recording device.

937. Visit a wax museum.

938. Own a *superball*!

939. And a recorder, (the kind that looks like a flute).

940. Have one of those human anatomy statues that show the inside of the body.

941. And an anatomy statue of an animal would be cool too.

942. Invent a secret handshake for you and your closest friend.

943. Every kid should own a Simon game.

944. And an hour glass.

945. Try to be an amateur ventriloquist.

946. Go to a Native Indian Pow-Wow.

947. Build a house of cards.

948. Take a ride in a rickshaw.

949. Learn how to walk with a book balanced on your head.

950. Visit a real lighthouse, (while there are any left).

951. Tour a real clipper-ship.

952. Own several pairs of colored sunglasses.

953. Every kid should own a water rocket.

954. It would be cool own a pair of toe socks.

955. Find a best friend, a real one. This can be one of the hardest things to do in life.

956. Don't obsess over material things. Your life is worth more than nice things to own. Even though I mention things in this book that it would be nice to have, if you don't, it doesn't really matter.

957. Learn not to be aggressive. People will tell you that violence is no answer to a problem. For the most part this is true, but also know when it is necessary, as it can be unrealistic to remain completely passive when in danger. Understand that you should not go around looking for a fight. But do defend yourself

or someone who is helpless if you must. And never use more force than is necessary if you can help it.

958. Learn to find your own way. There may be situations in life where you feel like you are owed something. Even if you are, you may never get it, so find your own way. You will get no-where in life waiting for a free ride. Those among us who have succeeded have done so by earning it. Earn your way through life, use your hands for guidance, not for begging.

959. Learn not to fear nature. Too many people are becoming afraid of the natural world, animals, insects, germs and bacteria. Most of these things are harmless. We were meant to be part of the natural world, we were not meant to hide from it.

960. Learn not to seek revenge. The best kind of revenge is success. If you are successful in life despite the people who may deliberately try to hold you back or hold you down, this is your true revenge. To be the best *you* you can be, regardless of hardships. And the best part is that the other people need never know, as long as you know you are successful, it is enough.

961. Learn to be independent. Go through life with the strength of knowing that when you are with someone, it is because you choose to

be, not because you cannot function without someone else controlling your life.

962. Try to find a job as soon as you are old enough. It does not matter what the job is as long as it is legitimate. It is an important lesson to experience honest work and earn your own money.

963. Compile a list of things you would like to do when you are grown.

964. And a list of places you would like to go.

965. You should have a list of professions of interest too.

966. Have at least a one year plan in place for your future.

967. And a five year plan to follow that, (plans can be changed to suit you as needed).

968. Have a dream for the future.

969. And a backup plan for that dream.

970. Review your college options early. Even if it is only a community college or vocational training, this can change your life.

971. Learn to make the best use of your time. All young people seem to want is to act or look older because they are in a hurry to be older, and all older people seem to want is to be young again because they were in such a hurry

when they were young that they made bad use of their time when they had it.

972. Learn to speak your language properly. No matter how smart you are you will always seem stupid to other people if they cannot understand what you are saying. This will slow down or even stop your progress in life. Speak slowly, clearly and without slang and profanity.

973. Learn to listen to the natural cues of your body. When you are healthy, if something is wrong your body knows how to tell you. It is an art that many have forgotten from childhood because they abuse themselves with poor diet and exercise.

974. Learn to eat in moderation. Your body knows what it needs and how much when you are healthy. When you force yourself to eat things that are not healthy and in larger quantities than your body should handle, you lose the ability to tell the difference.

975. Know the difference between real life and pretend life on television, people on television are actors, their lives are not real.

976. Know the difference between real life and imaginary life in video games, video game characters are imaginary, their lives are not real.

977. Study advertising. Understand what it does and why. The purpose of advertisement is to convince someone that they need or want something that they may not actually need or want. Learn not to be controlled by such influences.

978. Learn to decipher PC, (Politically Correct) language. This is a feel good language that is very often used to make something sound like something else that it is not. It is used by schools, businesses and government to make people feel good about something that may not be so nice. It is often dishonest and misleading because people miss the point when they do not understand the terms being used. Learn how to identify it, and do not be mislead by it. The truth is better, even if it hurts.

979. Have a mentor, preferably a parent if possible.

980. Learn not to gossip, gossiping about other people's problems makes their problems bigger and your mind smaller.

981. Listen more than you speak. You cannot learn if you are the one always talking.

982. Learn to keep a secret for a friend, and know how to tell the difference when it is a secret that *must* be told.

983. Learn to always be truthful. Honesty is very hard to come by.

984. And never lie to yourself; this is the worst kind of lie. Be who you are, not what you think others want you to be.

985. Always keep an open mind about other people's differences, even when they can't understand yours or you don't understand theirs, you don't have to understand someone to accept that they are different.

986. Learn to accept responsibility with dignity. Do not blame others for your own misfortunes, misbehaviors and misunderstandings.

987. Learn to accept criticism. Not all criticism is bad. Sometimes it is done in order to bring your attention to a fault so that it can be corrected. Although it is true that there are many that will use criticism to hurt you, this is not always the case. Know the difference between when it is coming from someone who is genuinely concerned for you and when it is coming from someone who is trying to insult you. Know how to take it, or how to ignore it.

988. Learn to accept failure with dignity. It is okay to not be first in everything every time. Every person is not a winner every time, and that is fine, that is natural and that inspires healthy

competition. People often spend so much time worrying about what they cannot do that they neglect what they can do.

989. Learn to never be a quitter. Just because you are not good at something the first time is no reason to give up if it is something that you really want to do. A very good musician for example may have to practice for ten years or more to be good and even longer to be great. You are going to be around that long anyway, use your time wisely.

990. Learn that you are not at the center of the world and that the entire universe does not revolve around you and what you want. We are each of us a very small speck in a picture that is so vast that we may never fully comprehend it. Although we are each of us important, we are not the most important single thing at every time.

991. Learn not to be a hypochondriac. Too many people grow up exaggerating everything that they do. If you are half an hour late getting lunch, you are not *starving*. If you go without any food at all for six weeks, then you are starving! Do not go through life as if every little inconvenience is a major disaster; this is a weakness to behave this way.

992. Learn not to nitpick. Everything can't be perfect and the way you want it all the time.

It is very selfish to be ungrateful when people are trying to help you or do you a favor.

993. Learn to understand the difference between wants and needs. Few people truly understand this difference and go through life being very selfish and unhappy.

994. Learn to make your own decisions. People who cannot make a decision in life have decisions made for them, and although this seems easier, having choices made for you because you are indecisive is not always a good thing.

995. Never give up on yourself. Everyone else can give up on you, but don't give up on yourself. Life is hard; the trick to life is to make it hard on your own terms, not on other people's terms. Do you think your favorite sports star got to be an MVP because they gave up on themselves because *training* six hours a day is hard? Do you think your favorite actor gets all those great parts because they don't want to spend ten hours a day in rehearsal?

996. Learn to be free of limitations. People setting limitations on themselves are their greatest weakness. Few people ever reach their potential because they convince themselves that they cannot do something before they even try.

997. Learn not to be cruel. If you have a problem then it is your problem. You must find a way either with help or on your own to master the problem. You cannot transfer your pain onto someone or something else, it isn't fair. If you are unhappy, it will not help you to torment another person or animal.

998. Learn not to harm yourself. You cannot solve a problem or remove emotional pain from your life by harming yourself or setting yourself up to be harmed. You will only become desensitized to this new sensation and continue it until you destroy yourself.

999. Understand that there is only one race, the human race. All people of any type or color are all hybrids of an original type of person that no longer exists. The same as all dogs are hybrids of the original type of dog, the wolf. If we were not all of one race, we would not be compatible with other nationalities. We are all a single species. The only true differences between people are social ones, religion, nationality, culture, language and so on. Not race. Since the differences are social, they are differences in our minds, and we can change our minds.

1000. Learn the power of *yes*. Do not be afraid of taking chances in life that could be a benefit to you or the ones you love because you are afraid of the unknown.

1001. Learn the power of *no*. It is through the power of no that I am what I am today, while nearly everyone that I grew up with, (literally) is dead, in jail, or homeless. While all of my peers were smoking, drinking, experimenting with drugs and unprotected sex, I said no. Those who were my friends understood, and those who tried to push me, well, they really weren't my friends, now were they?

The point is, live. Live, live, live, and enjoy life! Life is hard, but it doesn't have to be so hard all of the time! The moments are out there, you have to find them!